The Gift of Peace

Also by Ben Stein

HOW TO RUIN YOUR LIFE
(also available as an audio book)

HOW TO RUIN YOUR LOVE LIFE

HOW TO RUIN YOUR FINANCIAL LIFE

HOW TO RUIN . . . Book Collection
(comprises the three titles above)

All of the above are available at your local bookstore,
or may be ordered by visiting:
Hay House USA: **www.hayhouse.com**
Hay House Australia: **www.hayhouse.com.au**
Hay House UK: **www.hayhouse.co.uk**
Hay House South Africa: **orders@psdprom.co.za**

The Gift of Peace

Guideposts on the Road to Serenity

Ben Stein

HAY HOUSE, INC.
Carlsbad, California
London • Sydney • Johannesburg
Vancouver • Hong Kong

Published and distributed in the United States by: Hay House, Inc., P.O. Box 5100, Carlsbad, CA 92018-5100 • *Phone:* (760) 431-7695 or (800) 654-5126 • *Fax:* (760) 431-6948 or (800) 650-5115 • www.hayhouse.com • **Published and distributed in Australia by:** Hay House Australia Pty. Ltd., 18/36 Ralph St., Alexandria NSW 2015 • *Phone:* 612-9669-4299 • *Fax:* 612-9669-4144 • www.hayhouse.com.au • **Published and distributed in the United Kingdom by:** Hay House UK, Ltd. • Unit 62, Canalot Studios • 222 Kensal Rd., London W10 5BN • *Phone:* 44-20-8962-1230 • *Fax:* 44-20-8962-1239 • www.hayhouse.co.uk • **Published and distributed in the Republic of South Africa by:** Hay House SA (Pty), Ltd., P.O. Box 990, Witkoppen 2068 • *Phone/Fax:* 2711-7012233 • orders@psdprom.co.za • **Distributed in Canada by:** Raincoast • 9050 Shaughnessy St., Vancouver, B.C. V6P 6E5 • *Phone:* (604) 323-7100 • *Fax:* (604) 323-2600

Editorial supervision: Jill Kramer   *Design:* Amy Rose Szalkiewicz

Library of Congress Cataloging-in-Publication Data

Stein, Benjamin, 1944-
  The gift of peace : guideposts on the road to serenity / Ben Stein.
    p. cm.
  ISBN 1-4019-0514-5 (hardcover)
  1. Peace of mind--Religious aspects--Meditations. 2. Affirmations. I. Title.
  BL627.55.S74 2005
  204'.32--dc22

                              2004014140

                   ISBN 13: 978-1-4019-0514-9
                   ISBN 10: 1-4019-0514-5

                 08 07 06 05   4 3 2 1
                   1st printing, March 2005

Printed in the United States of America

For the men and women of Spiritual Search,
Point Dume, Malibu, 1988–1994 . . .
my apostles on the road to peace.

Introduction

In the late fall of 1987, I lost my way badly. I started hanging around with the wrong companions. I started taking too many prescription drugs (although always far less than the murderous amounts prescribed).

I was frantic with anxiety about eating too much and about my disastrously poor family relations—and I had the sickening sense that I was the villain, not the hero, of my life.

To make a long story short, two wonderful friends, Victoria Sackett and John Mankiewicz, suggested that I start going to meetings of various 12-step groups. I did, and they were a miracle.

In particular, one meeting I went to in the Point Dume area of Malibu was a lifesaver. It was at noon in a disused school that had been converted to a community center. Day after day I sat in that meeting and learned more about how to live my life than I had ever learned in college; in law school; or even from my brilliant mother and father, my incisive sister, and my close-to-perfect wife.

As I listened to the "sharing" by my brothers and sisters in that room, thoughts of peace and hope began to replace the hopelessness that I'd felt. I began to write down what I heard, and then, very soon, my own thoughts in similar veins began to come up, and I wrote them down as well.

My problems had never been entirely about medication or alcohol or food. They were about very confused and self-destructive thinking: believing that I was in charge of my life, that I was on trial all the time, and that God was an afterthought. The sincere feelings I heard being expressed in that room—and in many other like-minded rooms—made me realize that I had it all wrong. I was a tiny little bit player. God ran and *does* run the show. He doesn't want money or fame or success from me . . . just peace . . . and this is what I must want for myself if I have any sense at all—or even if I don't.

Without realizing when it actually happened, I began to become what I should have always been: a spiritual being having a human experience instead of the reverse. Little by little, a little bit of peace, and then more peace, came into my life. It's still incomplete. I'm a work in progress. I make a huge number of mistakes—personal, moral, and every other sort. I am a sinner in every possible area, and I torment myself and others still. God is far from finished with me yet, as the saying goes. But when I am on the road, when I am at home, when I am happy, when I am sad, when I am scared, when I am confident, I read these thoughts that I started to hear in the Point Dume meeting every day, and without fail they give me peace. Therefore, I am duty-bound to share them. I get most out of what I give away.

Without further ado, I offer the thoughts that I heard mostly at that noon meeting in Point Dume, and also in other similar rooms, many of them thoughts I heard in my own little head. I believe that taken regularly, they lead to what The Ancients called the greatest of all gifts: peace.

It is very possible that some of these thoughts have already appeared in printed form, were read by someone at the meetings and repeated, and then I took them down as original. I apologize in advance if I have written down what someone else already did. I also mention that there are a few lessons here that I consider so important that I have repeated them.

To make sure that others can receive this gift, I'm going to give all my proceeds after taxes and commissions to 12-step programs. They deserve it.

Good luck, and peaceful reading.

$$\sim\!\!\leftarrow\!\!\sim$$

1

When all else fails,
turn it over to God.

2

Fear underlies all my problems,
and my fear is a measure of how far
I am keeping myself from God.

3

I may not be much,
but I am all that I think about.

4

My real dilemma:
I can never get enough of what
I don't even need.

5

Nothing fails like excess.

6

My life is and always has
been unmanageable by me.
But it's child's play for God.

7

If it can be fixed with money,
it is not a big problem.

8

I am a person made of the seven
deadly sins, and I always will be.
I'm not surprised by it. It's
called "being human."

9

If I have any sense at all, I have
to realize that I have what I need,
even if I don't have what I want.

10

Fear has been my Higher Power
for too much of my life.
Prayer is better.

11

One day at a time is the
answer to everything.

12

Luckily for me,
God works by mercy,
not by justice.

13

God lives in the results.
I live in the little baby steps.

14

Envy is a poisonous way of
measuring my distance from God.

15

There is only one real
type of wealth: peace of mind.

16

It is great to tell others to
surrender to God, but far better
to surrender yourself.

17

Fear is the common
human condition.
Faith is the solution.

18

I am not a good manager
of my own life, but God
is the perfect Boss.

19

What happens to me
is not very important.

20

I cannot control other people,
and when I try, it leads
to catastrophe.

21

I get exhausted trying to figure
out life. I cannot, so I'll just
turn it over to God today.

22

I am accepted by God,
and that's the best club in town.

23

Life is a lot like French toast.
If you don't turn it over, it burns.

24

Acceptance of what God
sends me is not a choice.
It is a necessity.

25

Not killing myself is up to me . . .
not to anyone else.

26

My main possession
is my love of God.

27

God will give me peace
if I give myself peace.

28

The only real healing
comes from God.

29

When I surrender to God,
I like me.

30

Acceptance is the
only choice I have.
It's not even a choice.
It's a necessity.

31

Angry, fearful, and lonely
is no way to go through life.
Trusting God is the best way
to go through life.

32

I am not here to change the world.
I am here to be changed.

33

The problem is
my powerlessness.
The solution is also
my powerlessness.

34

The whole meaning of God is that
He loves you and forgives
you for being human.

35

Surrendering to God
is not giving up.
It is moving to the
winning side.

36

Let's face facts.
We are going to have some bad days.
That is life.

37

Put your trust in God and go
on with your day's work.
That is health.

38

I would rather be
comfortable than right.

39

I am going to forgive myself
as much as I forgive others.

40

I think that today I will stay
away from people who are
foreseeably harmful.

41

Whatever I am going through,
others have gone through it
with God's help.

42

Today I will live
in faith instead of fear.

43

My job today is to do a bit
of work and stay calm and not
hurt anyone, including myself.
That's it.

44

Thank you, God, for allowing
me to realize that what is going
on in my head is not what is
going on in my real life.

45

Sometimes the other shoe
simply does not drop.

46

You can cut your throat over
a broken shoelace or turn it
over to God and stay calm.

47

The answer to every
problem and every issue is:
God's will be done.

48

Self-pity is a prison.
I want out.

49

Don't obsess about money—
if you have enough,
that is enough.

50

When in fear,
consult with reality.

51

Today I am
not going to judge—
not even myself.

52

Life can be faced by doing
something or by complaining.
It is up to you.

Instead of trying to figure out
the universe, try to think about
what you want for lunch.

I do not care to spend
today in self-loathing.

55

I have never been stepped
on by an elephant, but the fleas
drive me crazy.

56

God put me here, and this
means I have the right to be here.

57

If I am getting upset
over something that would
not bother most people,
I am getting too upset.

58

You really cannot lose
if you stay on your
knees and pray.

59

I can go crazy thinking
about the future, or I can stay
calm thinking about now.

60

Start each day with
gratitude and that
day works better.

61

If I begin the day by thanking God for my eyes, my ears, my mouth, my legs, my arms, my heart, my lungs, my being in a free country, my having a roof over my head and plenty to eat, nothing that happens to me later in the day counts for much.

62

I am not The Director of the movie of my life. That is a Power far greater than I will ever be.

63

I am just one bit player in the
world's drama today, and to think
I am the prima donna of that movie
is an invitation to insanity.

64

What happens to me today is just
what happens in one person's life
out of eight billion people on Earth.
This should give me some perspective
on just how big my problems are.

65

We have to pray for those
who harm us, but we also have
to avoid them if at all possible.

66

Life is precious—even my life.

67

I am a human among humans,
a worker among workers, a sufferer
among sufferers, a child among
children, a loser among losers,
a winner among winners, but
always a child of God.
And that is plenty.

68

It is not hard to feel gratitude
when you're feeling good. It is hard
to feel it when you're feeling bad.
That is called "life."

69

Life is filled with unresolved
problems. That is another
reason it's called "life."

70

Why not be as generous
to yourself as you would
be to a good friend?

71

Life should be like
matchmaking a relationship
with God.

72

I am not the boss of anything,
especially not my family.

73

Surrender works—
but this means surrender to God,
not necessarily to man.

74

Why not just do the best
you can and let God
handle the results?

75

The absolutely shortest,
surest way to peace is to fall to your
knees and ask God for help and
surrender to whatever God decides.

76

Feelings come and feelings go.

77

Feelings are not facts.

78

Maybe if I have a lot of problems
I should be grateful, because it
shows that my life is full.

79

I think that right now
I will make a list of
what I have that I like,
not what I don't have
that I want.

80

I am a diversified holding
company, and my number one
asset is trust in God.

81

If I start each day with
a list of all that I have just by
being born and living in America,
I would spend the whole day
doing it, and it would
be a good day.

82

I cannot afford to spend all
my time judging everyone
and everything around me.
It hurts me, and it hurts
everyone near me.

83

It is worth repeating the question:
Do you want to live by fear or by faith?
The question is so simple
that it answers itself.

84

When I am in doubt, I try to think
about how Gary Cooper would have
handled it, and that often
works pretty well.

85

When I am agitated and in fear,
maybe I need to rest and eat,
not fight and conquer or die.

86

I feel a lot better if I stay out of
expectations and stay in the now.

87

Expectations are predetermined
disappointments. Stay away from
them if you can.

88

We are all mortals. We start with
that and we go on with our lives,
but we should not be
surprised by it.

89

Fear is my mortal enemy.
I have to avoid it, and when
I am afflicted with it, I pray over it.

90

I do not want to be alone in my head.
I want to have God and my family
and friends with me when
I am alone.

91

My goal is not wealth or fame.
My goal is peace, which is
the only true wealth.

92

I have only one life on Earth.
I do not choose to waste it in
self-loathing and envy and fear.

93

To me, envy is as deadly as cyanide,
and I have to avoid it just as surely
as I avoid drinking poison.

94

I want to be like the Strategic
Air Command and have *peace*
as my profession.

95

I do not care to fight
about who is right or wrong.
I just want to be in a state of peace.

96

There is always some
damned thing that can upset us.
The variable is our serenity.
We cannot control the world,
but we *can* control our serenity.

97

God has always taken care of me,
and I am foolish to believe
He will stop now.

98

Look at your life: How little
of it did you plan or control,
and how much just happened
to you? Then how can you
doubt that God is running
your life for your benefit?

99

Anger is a lot like loneliness:
self-inflicted wounds that take
too long to heal. Leave it alone.

100

My primary weapon is prayer.

101

Faith is my road map.

102

My relationships work about
as well as I work them, and
this is especially true of the
main one—the one with God.

103

Time brings changes but
not necessarily *good* changes.
Prayer and rest make
for good changes.

104

Change rarely hurts,
but resistance to change
is a killer.

105

The delusion that I run
my life entirely is
almost funny.

106

A simple test: What I want
to happen is *my* will.
What *happens* is God's will.
I will accept it.

107

By any fair standard,
I have far more than
I deserve or need.

108

God is not my servant.
He is my Master.

109

My mind is a terrifying place
to be alone in, especially
in the morning. I need
to ask God to come
stay with me.

110

When you truly surrender,
you get out of God's way and
He can do his work *for* you
and *on* you.

111

You are always safe
when you are in gratitude.

112

I am allowed to complain,
and I am allowed to throw a fit,
but then I will come back to the
safe harbor of gratitude.

113

God did not make man perfect.
That means I am allowed
to fail not only occasionally
but frequently.
Only God does not fail.

114

It is insanity to believe
that my mistakes are very
important in the way of the world.

115

I do not have to please any
of the critics in my head. It is not
my job to make imaginary
people happy.

116

You can hang yourself
anywhere or save
yourself anywhere.

117

You can learn by being quiet
as well as by talking.

118

My goal today is to be
calm and trust in God.

119

It is good to have a vision
of who you want to be.

120

The person who is afraid
is a part of me, but it is not
the *only* part of me.

121

Winning or losing
is not a moral issue.

122

I need God holding
my hand every minute of every day.

123

I do not have to serve people
just because they ask me to.

124

If I get angry at myself, that does
not help anybody or anything.

125

I think that maybe I need
to make a list of what I am satisfied
about, not what I am griping about.

126

If I begin every day by just
throwing in the towel and accepting
what God sends my way, that day
works pretty well.

127

Do not bother to ask God for what
you want. Ask Him to show
you what He wants.

128

When someone or something
hurts you, try to get well,
not hurt yourself more.

129

All real power comes from
surrendering to God's will.

130

God is always there,
and His will is always working,
no matter what you think.

131

Acceptance means accepting
everything—including what
you don't like just as much
as what you do like.

132

When agitated and in fear,
just imagine that God is
saying to you, "Be still and
know that I am God."

133

What other people think
about me is none of my business.
How I behave toward them
is entirely my business.

134

A good way to begin your day
is to be grateful for your fingers,
your toes, your ears, your eyes,
your hands, your life, and from
then on, nothing seems
that important.

135

My bad thoughts about
you don't hurt you—they hurt me.

136

My relationship with God is the
only relationship that counts, and
if it's right, all other relationships
in my life will be right, no matter
how they turn out.

137

Whatever the impossible
problem in your life,
let go and let God,
and the problem goes away.

138

Many people cannot walk.
I could always walk. I just never
knew where I was going.

139

I was teachable this morning,
and that makes it a good morning.
Be teachable, and you'll get
where you are supposed
to be in one piece.

140

The less I think I am in control,
the more I acknowledge that God
is in control, and the better I feel.

141

Most people are introduced to
God by other people who are not
happy, and they make God in that
image. But that's not God.
God is love.

142

The test of serenity is having
to absorb someone else's anger.
The solution is to turn it over
to God, to simply let it go.

143

When we quit blaming people
other than ourselves for our problems,
we make giant steps toward serenity.

144

You have to go through pain
to get to the other side.

145

One of the worst nightmares
you can have is to imagine that
you die from your craziness and
that you then get to see how great
your life would have been if you
had just surrendered to God.

146

Freedom is the realization
that there's the way things are
and the way they should be in
your mind, and the two are
never going to be the same.

147

All serious long-term pain
in the mind is caused by the
avoidance of legitimate suffering.

148

You cannot think your way
into right acting. You can only
act your way into right thinking.

149

The only things I absolutely
have to do today are to not hurt
myself and not hurt anyone else
and to surrender to God's will.

150

I am never going to be perfect.
I am never going to wake up one
morning and from then on never
make a mistake. At the very best,
I will be a human being . . . but a
human being surrendered to God.

151

There is a movie going on. It is called
"Life—the Movie". . . . I am just one
bit player in a cast of billions. God is
the Director of that movie, not me.

152

We didn't create ourselves,
and all we create when we try to
take charge is a lot of confusion.

153

Why don't I just step out of my
head and let God love me?

154

Why do we hurt ourselves?
What happens is beyond
our control anyway.

155

Every problem is a good reason
and avenue to get closer to God.

156

What you have to unlearn to get
to peace and serenity is every
bit as important as what
you have to learn.

157

How fast can you get out of pain?
As fast as you can
truly surrender.

158

Even when things are bleakest,
when I have been completely pushed
against the wall, I can still surrender.
I always have that much strength.

159

If I learn to clean up my house,
God will love you through me.

160

The perfect time is now.

161

For years, I was crazy and suffering. It never occurred to me that I was suffering because I was acting crazy. Yet when I stopped acting crazy, the suffering stopped.

162

When I am in pain, it is usually because I have hurt myself.

163

Life is a series of unresolved problems—not just for me, but for everyone.

164

The best thought I used to have
was that I was not good enough.
That is a total waste of time.

165

Feelings Come and Feelings Go,
and Feelings Are Not Facts:
Carve it in stone.

166

Almost every problem I face
is right between my ears.

167

Today I will take everyone
else off the hook and take
responsibility for all that I did.

168

Today I will accept what is.

169

When you do something good
for someone you don't
care for, it's for God,
not for that person.

170

It is amazing how little
of our thinking each day
is based on reality.

171

Pain is the touchstone of growth.

172

"Surrender" is derived from
the French phrase *"Se rendre,"*
to "offer yourself up"—
and surrender works because
we offer ourselves
up to God.

173

We are as sick as our secrets.

174

When God talks to us,
He talks through other people
who have gone through what we
have gone through and have
survived and triumphed.

175

Clarity about who
we are hurts at first, then helps.

176

There is no such thing
as a life without problems.
The only variable is our serenity.
It is worth hearing twice.

177

The secret of getting through
anything is that, in the end,
everything is going to be all right.
We will be with God.

178

I don't have to know all the
answers today. I don't have to be
brilliant and decisive today. I just
have to go through the day.

179

I need to focus on what's right today,
and if I do, I get through the pain
and don't cause anyone else pain.

180

My life does not have to be an endless
punishment filled with self-criticism.

181

Relax.
You're not in charge.
God is.
He does good work.

182

There is no excuse not to love.

183

Sometimes you're riding on top
of the wave and sometimes you're
under the wave. It's always where
you're supposed to be.

184

If you don't live in expectations,
you get to avoid disappointment.

185

Do not expect equal sharing
of burdens every day.

186

It is not a catastrophe or a historical
tragedy if your day does not go
as planned. It's called "life."

187

Any smart person can
justify anything. That does
not make it right.

188

If you share your pain,
that cuts the pain in half.

189

If you stay out of results,
you get great results.

190

Feeling lonely is like having
your feelings be hungry.
Feed them with service
to others and with love.

191

When I'm not where
I'm comfortable, I'm uncomfortable.
This is a bit more important
than it sounds.

192

Why do you have to be the best
at anything? Why put yourself under
that burden? Why not just be
good enough? Leave perfectionism
to someone else.

193

God is always there for me.
I just have to be there for Him.

194

There are people who make
excuses and there are people
who take action.

195

You don't expect anyone else
to be perfect. Why expect yourself
to be perfect?

196

Perfectionism is just
another useless, harmful
form of self-obsession.

197

Your life need not be an
endless session of fault-finding
with yourself and others.

198

When I accept God's will that
we are all supposed to be different,
I make life a lot easier on everyone.

199

On the road between the drunks
and the dolphins, we learn from
the drunks *and* the dolphins.

200

My job is to keep
my little corner
of the world clean.

201

It is not my job to keep track
of other people or tell them
how to live their lives.

202

Inner peace keeps
me connected with
the whole universe.

203

I don't have to go out and
steal something or be somebody
famous to be part of the universe.
I'm already a part of it
just by being here.

204

I am present for my own
life today if I stay calm.

205

There is a Consciousness out there.
I am not the only consciousness
in the universe.

206

The only reality that exists
for me today is spirituality.

207

I do not have to know the answers
to every question. I just have to
know enough to turn it over to God.
That's the only answer I need to know.

208

Say it to yourself over and over
throughout the day: *Turn it over,
turn it over, turn it over.*

209

At some point you have
to call a truce in the war
against yourself.

210

Every bad and good thing
that happens is a way and an
opportunity to get closer to God.

211

When people beat you up,
you need not feel that you have
to join in and beat yourself up, too.

212

I do not have time in my
life for resentment. If I waste
my time on resentment,
I do not have time for joy.

213

If someone hurts my feelings,
I just say "Ouch!" and
go on with my day.

214

When in pain, stay in the moment.
If you can stay in the now, you can
get through anything.

215

It does not matter what you
think of me. It only matters
that I am surrendered to God.

216

He who lives with
the most surrender wins.

217

God did not go away on
vacation and leave me in charge.

218

If I can just connect with the gift
of being alive, I can feel gratitude
today and immediately
feel comfortable.

219

I can plan attempts,
but I cannot plan results.

220

When I am restless, irritable,
or discontent, I know I am not
in the right place.

221

What I see as my
greatest weaknesses, others may
see as my greatest strengths.

222

Life is not all punishment.
It is largely opportunity if you are
looking with the eyes of faith.

223

The best things in my life
have very little to do
with money.

224

Try to think of the worst, most upsetting things that happened to you years ago. You probably cannot even remember them.

225

I am a lot better at lying, especially to myself, than I am at telling the truth. This, too, is called "being human."

226

For most of my life I had a simple test: Right was what I wanted. Wrong was not getting it.

227

Conscious prayer will
work miracles. If you pray
before trying to lift a heavy
rock, you can lift it.

228

You solve problems if you live
in the solution. You do not solve
them if you live in the problem.

229

The power of resentment
hurts everyone. The power
of forgiveness helps
everyone.

230

Other people were not placed
on Earth for my convenience or
just to serve me. Other people
have their own lives, duties, hopes,
fears, and motivations totally
independent of me and
beyond my control.

231

I am not responsible for the
operation of the universe today.

232

No one gets everything done
in a day that he wants to get done.
That is called "life."

233

I have a choice today about whether to be crazy or sane. Sane means taking it easy. Insane means self-obsession. I think I know which one I'll choose today.

234

You do not need to carry around other people's stress.

235

Stay in the moment—the warm, soothing pool of the moment.

236

Maybe I should just decide what
movie I would like to see today
instead of whether or not
I should kill myself.

237

Do I want to live? If so, I had
better accept life on life's terms.

238

The me who can forgive
is truly walking with God.

239

Just to be alive is to be rich.

240

Put away the stick and
stop beating yourself up.

241

You can't think yourself
into doing right. Just do
right and you'll feel right.

242

Faith is the eye of the hurricane.

243

There is a magic potion.
It is faith in God.

244

You don't have to do anything to fit
in with God's crowd except
to believe in Him.

245

If we believe,
He will take care of us,
no matter what we think
He is doing.

246

We are all each other's servants
if we are smart about it, but
not each other's doormats.

247

Faith is greater
than fear if you work at it.

248

If you want to improve the show,
try firing yourself as director.

249

I am not ever going to be perfect
or even close to it. Why even
bother to try?

250

There is only one problem,
which includes all other problems.
That problem is fear.
There is one solution to it:
Turn your life over to God.

251

My life is the sum total of what
I have done about it until now,
including surrendering it.

252

Maybe my decision for today
should be to just do what's in front
of me instead of trying to take
over the universe.

253

When we judge others,
we are really judging ourselves.

254

When you keep yourself serene,
you are getting a foretaste of heaven.

255

A humble but liberating thought:
When other people have a thought
that is different from mine, maybe
they are right and I am wrong.

256

When people criticize me,
maybe they are right and I am wrong.
I won't die if I admit it.

257

Anything that goes wrong
in our lives can be taken care of
by prayer, rest, nutrition, and not
hurting anyone, including
ourselves.

258

Other people judge us by our
actions, not our intentions.

259

I do not have to waste my time
today speculating on other
people's motives. I embrace them
if they are kind and avoid them
if they are mean.

260

I surrender to what happens today
and accept it even when—
especially when—it is not
what I wanted.

261

If I am going to make any
difference at all in the world today,
it must start with my actions.

262

You may be insane—
and we all are—but if we do not
act upon that insanity, we will
not get into trouble.

263

Life is not so short that we
do not have time to consider
the views of others.

264

I do not have to know enough
to get it all together. All I have
to do is know enough to
ask God for help.

265

I don't think I will be
my own worst enemy today.

266

If we use people as drugs,
we will get the same results
as if we used drugs.

267

I do not want to even get out
of bed this morning without
being in God's will and
accepting that lucky fate.

268

The best mantra
is simply "faith."

269

When people say I am wrong,
sometimes they are right and
sometimes I am wrong. To be
wrong is not a capital crime.

270

There are limits on what I can
do, be, or accomplish today.
This is what it means to be
a human being.

271

Today, maybe if I am wise,
I will gather myself and my friends
together and stop hurting myself.

272

Stress is a basic part of human life,
but with God's help, it does not
have to be a permanent part of life.

273

You are always safe when
you are in gratitude.

274

When I am alone in my head, I am in
the most dangerous neighborhood in
America, far worse than any gangster
neighborhood. I want to stay in the best
neighborhood in town—the 'hood of
gratitude, surrender, and prayer.

275

I am sane if I know I am
allowed to make mistakes, but
insane if I think my mistakes
are very important.

276

Get busy living, not dying.

277

You learn from talking
and also from being quiet.

278

It is good to have a vision
of who you want to be.
My vision is to be calm
and trust in God.

279

It's a funny thing, but I cannot
handle life in any more of
a piece than 24 hours a day.

280

Winning or losing
is not a moral issue.

281

I am just a child when
it comes to fear: I need God
holding my hand every
second of every day.

282

I do not have to serve
people just because they
ask me to do so.

283

You don't get paid unless
you work; you don't get serenity
unless you work at it.

284

God does not have to go through me to reach the people He wants to help, but I am lucky if I make it easy for Him to do so.

285

Just leave it alone is often very, very good advice.

286

I am afflicted with the human condition of mortality and fear and will be until I die.

287

"I'm sorry" is good.
Not doing it in the first
place is better.

288

There is only one really
big idea: that if we all want,
we can be connected with God.

289

It is good to avoid sick, angry
people. I really cannot fix them,
but they can hurt me.

290

If I get into a fight with someone, I hurt because I carry him or her around with me in my head all day, so I lose no matter what.

291

Three simple rules of having a better day: *Rest, meditate, do what's right.*

292

It is often a good idea to think, *What's normal?* and then try to do that.

293

Life is an endless
learning experience—for everyone.

294

Thoughts I have when
I am well rested are entirely
different and better than thoughts
I have when I am exhausted.

295

If I have enough to make it
through the day, I think I will
stop worrying about tomorrow.

296

A novel idea: Maybe we should talk to the people we have issues with and listen to what they say.

297

It is a good day when I realize that God loves me just as I am.

298

I think I will no longer fight the inevitable, at least not today.

299

Simple actions lead to simple good habits, which leads to good character.

300

Just for this one day, I think I will go on a vacation from fear.

301

Just for this one day, I think I will go on a vacation from envy.

302

Just for this one day, I think
I will accept that I am a human being
with limitations and weaknesses.

303

This is life. It is not a movie.
And I am not an invulnerable
superhero. I am just a human being
with all of a human being's failings,
and if I accept that about myself,
I am far ahead of the game.

304

My imagination is
one of my greatest assets
and also my greatest liability.

305

The best of the human condition:
to keep losing and yet keep in
the game, knowing that staying
in the game is winning.

306

In the bad times,
fear is my Higher Power.

307

I am well off when God is
my Higher Power, and those
are the good times.

308

It is worth saying over
and over again: It is vitally important
to be rested—not just rested,
but *well* rested.

309

All the power I have comes from
admitting my own powerlessness.

310

God is my Father, my Boss,
my Best Friend.

311

Prayer works . . . and prayer
works wonders.

312

Just for today, I will not bully
or threaten anyone, but I will
defend myself.

313

I have spent most of my life whining
and complaining and being in fear.
What a tragic waste of life.

314

Why not try one hour,
then one day, without fear?

315

When I emerge blinking from
the cavern of my fear, I have to
admit that I'm a very lucky person.

316

I do not have to be happy
every day, and to believe I have
to be happy every day is a
major burden.

317

I can be low or sad or gloomy
for a while, and maybe that is just
a form of rest. Anyway, I am
allowed to feel how I feel.

318

When I get to a place
where I have been content,
I should go back there.

319

Praise God is the answer
to a lot of issues, and the single
best thing you can do with your
mouth and your brain.

320

We do belong.
We are here and we belong.
God put us here.

321

The enemy is not "out there"—
he's "in here." The enemy
is my own self-doubt
and self-destruction.

322

Self-loathing is far worse
than being in a room
full of cockroaches.

323

Stay in the warm pool
of faith, trust, hope, and love.
That pool will be calm and safe
and warm no matter what. And if
it's a really good pool, it will
also have friends in it.

324

I am a slave to fear, and when
I am a slave, I am in bad shape.
It is better to be in faith and to be free.

325

If I believe that God loves me
with all my faults and no matter
what I do, then I am incredibly calm.

326

It is morning and it is a great day
and let's get on with it—do our work
and live and let live—not halfway,
but the whole way.

327

We are what we do,
and this includes doing our prayers.

328

We are all victims of ourselves—
or beneficiaries of ourselves.

329

A great pianist does not have
to think about his past failures
every time he hits a key, and
neither do we every day we get up.

330

I do not have to believe what
other people tell me, but my critics
are often my best teachers.

331

When I touch anger, it is like
touching a high-tension wire—
I get burned.

332

Here is a basic truth:
We can change; life will not.

333

I am going to break a little
or a lot each day, but then I will
trust God to put me back together.

334

I was not born knowing
how to "do life," and the best
I can do is surrender
to God's will.

335

I will be a lot better off
if I surrender sooner
rather than later.

336

Man and woman are deeply
influenced by their surroundings—
when I surround myself with
the beauty of nature, I am
ahead of the game.

337

There are no destinations,
only the journey, and if you stay
on the road and enjoy the scenery,
you are doing fine.

338

I will not play the cassette of
self-hatred and terror today.
Instead, I will play the sweet
music of trust in God.

339

I do not have to
believe what other people tell me.

340

I do not have to self-destruct.
I can if I want to, but why
should I want to?

341

Surrender or die of anxiety
is a simple, clear way of looking
at the way to peace.

342

We are all victims of ourselves.

343

The enemy is not out there.
He is in here, in my head, in my
self-doubt and self-destruction,
but faith in God lets the enemy
out into a cloud of dust.

344

Let go and let God. That is always
the answer. Say it a hundred times
a day until it becomes
a part of you.

345

Maybe today I will not
be a terrorist against myself
or anyone else. I don't need
to blow up anything or anyone
to make a good day.

346

I do not have to be happy every day.
I do not have to be enthusiastic
every day. I am allowed to just
be quiet some days.

347

To build a relationship
is a lot better than
to destroy one.

348

Life is in session.
You will only learn
if you are awake.

349

All power comes from the
admission of powerlessness
before God.

350

Enemies are often
our best teachers.

351

I spend far too much time
complaining and not enough time
praising. I think it is time
for a change.

352

A bad day is not an excuse
to hate or rage against man or God.
Bad days are a standard part of life.

353

Why not try a Fear Holiday,
where you just leave fear behind?

354

Just for today, I think
I would rather drink arsenic
than engage in envy.

355

Maybe I have to step back
today and ask, "Am I really turning
my problems over to God?"

356

If I make myself
a channel of God's love,
I am having a great day.

357

My life is a gift. I was drowning,
and God threw me a life jacket.

358

To be loved,
you have to be lovable.

359

"Cool it" is often a good prescription
for daily life and for almost all
the problems of the moment.

360

Slow to speak, slow to anger,
fast to listen: that is
my goal today.

361

I am in this life to get lessons.
Life is a learning experience.

362

A good's night's sleep is a miracle
for determining how I feel.

363

If you want to play detective,
try to find the good
in every situation.

364

When you are stuck on the freeway,
or when you are in line waiting,
use this time as an opportunity
to feel gratitude.

365

Imagine how good you would
feel if you truly felt you were doing
what God wants you to do.

366

It is good to avoid envious people.
I cannot fix them, and they will
hurt me if they can.

367

I don't want someone
who doesn't like me to occupy
space rent-free in my head.

368

The Kingdom of
God is within.

369

"Just keep your mouth shut"
solves a lot of problems.

370

I am extremely fallible.
But God is always there to help
if I ask Him into my life and
surrender to Him.

371

What a gift: to be able
to live in the solution and
not the problem.

372

I will say it again:
There are no big deals except
to surrender to God.

373

Just for today,
I will detach from
difficult personalities.

374

Live life on life's terms?
It seems impossible, but with God,
it's very possible indeed.

375

My life is like a Rubik's Cube.
The parts don't fit together
unless faith is added.

376

I am powerless over fear,
and surrendering to that
powerlessness gives
me strength.

377

I am powerless over results.

378

It is not my job to be happy.
God has not promised me that
I will be happy. It is just my job
to be thankful and serve Him.

The person who is afraid
is a part of me. I should
just admit it.

I do not have to use up my day
being an unpaid servant to people
just because they ask me to.

381

If I get angry at myself, that does
not help anyone or anything.

382

There are stock market crashes
and real estate crashes, but there
are no faith-in-God crashes if you
are in the sunshine of faith.

383

I do not have to spend my day
pleasing invisible people in my head.

384

You can hardly ever
go wrong just doing
what is in front of you.

385

It is good to have
a vision of who you want to be.

386

I want to be
a calm person
who trusts in God.

387

The best address
in town is in the neighborhood
of gratitude and prayer.

388

I am allowed to complain.

389

I am allowed to throw a fit . . .
but I am not sure what
good it does me.

390

I am allowed to fail and
make mistakes, but it is insanity
to believe that my mistakes
are terribly important.

391

I am a human being. This is the
source of a lot of my problems.

392

The beast is within.
Only a partnership between
God and me can tame this beast.

393

The truth is that I am a
wreck without God and
a whole person *with* God.

394

God is totally willing to save
me if I am willing to save myself.

395

If I do my day's
work with God,
that day works.

396

The best morning exercise
you can do is to get out of bed
and get to your knees and ask
God to allow you to accept what
He throws your way that day—
in gratitude.

397

Don't ask God for what
you want; ask Him for what
He wants for you.

398

Will this action save my life?
That is the goal: to save my life.

399

Begin at once,
and do the best you can.

400

*Sit down and shut up
and pray* is the answer to
a great many things.

401

God put me here on Earth.
That means I have a place here
and do not have to apologize
for being me.

402

When I'm hurt,
I want to get well,
not hurt myself more.

403

You'd better surrender
or you're going to
be *forced* to surrender.

404

There is no one who is too stupid
to surrender to God, but there are
some who are too smart.

405

You get an immediate
result from surrender
and from service.

406

I will not melt away
if I let go of my
character defects.

407

You're in God's hands
no matter what
you think.

408

God is either everything
or He is nothing in my life.

409

Life requires
acceptance of everything—
not just what I care
to accept.

410

Acceptance = surrender.

141

411

There is little value
in self-pity.

412

There is no value
in not having faith.

413

Lower emotional
overhead is a major way
to save my life.

414

We just have to go
until we go to sleep.
There is no tomorrow.

415

Often, when we are
most desperate, we have
to believe there is no tomorrow.

416

The key word for today
is "We" = God and me.

417

Be still and
know that He is God.

418

If you let other people dictate
how you feel about yourself,
you might as well be a slave.

419

Every problem and every
struggle is a chance to
get closer to God.

420

I am not in control
today or any day.
Not of much.

421

My relationship
with God counts for everything.

422

Let go and let God—say it often
and the pain goes away.
You can't say it often enough.

423

Often, all we have is God,
which is all we need.

424

You can't figure anything out.
It's all God's will,
and it's known to Him, and
that's plenty to know.

425

Happiness is the
absence of unhappiness.

426

There are too many people
in my head yelling at me, and I think
I will let them just talk to each other.

427

God loves me whether
I win or lose, and I love Him
whether I win or lose.

428

Unless I am totally crazy,
I do not think I am God.
I am a servant of God,
and that is enough.

429

Faith has to be in something
permanent and reliable, and
that means not in people,
places, or things.
Faith must be in God.

430

I don't think I want
to be my own torturer and
Gestapo any longer.

431

I don't think I will launch
any surprise attacks against
myself today.

432

I can be serene for a long time
until I have to absorb someone's anger.
It's best to avoid such angry people.

433

Joy is a living, organic creature,
and when joy comes to visit,
I will be grateful.

434

I am sick and tired
of being sick and tired.

435

Alone is not the same as lonely.
Sometimes being alone with
God on our minds is the
best place to be.

436

What happens to me
is not terribly important.
I know I have said it before.

437

Just for today, I will not think
I am better than anyone else.

438

Just for today,
I will not think it is up to me
to change the world.

439

Just for a few minutes,
I will not be afraid.
Instead of a coffee break,
I will take a freedom-
from-fear break.

440

Just for today,
I will not drown out my body.
Instead, I will listen to it.

441

It is a great thing to know that there's
the way things are supposed to be
and the way they are, and the
two are rarely the same.

442

The bottom line is
that we are all God's kids.

443

The perfect place is right here,
and the perfect time is right now.

444

This is worth hearing a few times:
It's not about thinking yourself into
right acting. It's about acting your
way into right thinking.

445

If it's impossible,
it's probably because you think
it's impossible.

446

If it's possible, it's probably
because you think it's possible.

447

If I sincerely place
the welfare of others
ahead of mine,
I have no problems.

448 °

Let there be light.

449

Don't let the problem
be your Higher Power.

450

Envy leads to anger and depression.
Gratitude leads to happiness,
energy, and achievement.

451

God is in the now.
He's not in the future.
He's in the now.

452

There are no big deals, and
the number of people at my funeral
is none of my business.

453

The only things I have to do
today are not beat myself up,
not hurt anyone, and surrender to
God's will. That makes a full day.

454

When I start to count my faults,
the list is almost endless.
This offers a certain humility,
and we all need humility.

455

This is just a way station.

456

Fear can sometimes keep us
from doing stupid things—alas,
it can also keep us from
doing smart things.

457

Getting close to God, and
meditating and praying, are the
cures for my disease. I have to take
them every day.

458

We didn't create ourselves, and
when we act alone, without God,
all we create is a lot of confusion.

459

Life goes on.
Whatever you're involved in,
it's going to change.

460

I get angry when I am scared.
When I am at peace and in touch
with God, I am calm and forgiving.

461

I don't know what's best for me.
Only God knows that.
But if I get out of His way,
He will give it to me.

462

When you're meditating
and getting in touch with God,
it's like you're mainlining
inspiration.

463

I love to beat up on myself,
but then I am going to surrender
and feel better and wonder why
I did it in the first place.

464

God wants to help
with every problem.

465

My "lifestyle" should be
about being with people I love
and in places where I am
comfortable—not about cars
or houses or money.

466

Don't take any of it too seriously.

467

The entire business
of life is to forgive, including
forgiving ourselves.

468

Two keys to freedom:
Don't judge, and *Look for the
good and praise it.*

469

Treat your friends the way
you would treat great paintings:
See them in their best light.

470

An awful lot of what we think
is right is not right. We have
to unlearn and then
learn again.

471

Just for today I am going
to the delightful islands
of "surrender" and "acceptance."

472

As quick as I can surrender
and know that it's all God's will,
I really start to feel better.

473

I will get done today
what I *can* get done without
making myself frantic and crazy,
and that's plenty.

474

I hope that what I do
today may make the world
a slightly better place.

475

As bleak as things may be,
I can still surrender. I still have
that little bit of good sense—
to surrender to God's will
and refrain from fighting it.

476

My main lesson
has to be to learn to love.

477

Just for today
I would like to be content to be me.

478

Pain is often the difference
between what we want and
what is happening.

479

Too much excitement
is as bad for me as too much
alcohol or drugs or poison.

480

The perfect space and time
is here and now.

481

In a free society, we create our
own reality. It can be a reality of
faith or a reality of foolishness.

482

If you can't laugh at yourself,
you are missing the biggest
joke of all.

483

It is in my power
to stop hurting myself.

484

The answer
to much of my life is:
"It's none of my business."

485

Genius and happiness
are falling in love with
what we already have.

486

It is an amazing truth,
but if you dress cheerfully,
you will feel cheerful.

487

I have to go to God as if
I were a little child and say,
"I don't know what to do now.
Please guide me."

488

It is an amazing thing that
when I do things that are
foreseeably harmful to me,
they actually turn out
to *be* harmful.

489

I have to repeat this over and over:
I am not going to compare my insides
with other people's outsides.

490

We are not all supposed
to be the same. I do not have
to be the same as anyone else.

491

"God's will be done" is the
answer to everything difficult
that happens in the world, no matter
how impossible it seems.

492

So what if our backs
are against the wall?
God is our wall.

493

It is worth reading again:
Feelings come and feelings go,
and feelings are not facts.

494

Why don't I take everyone
else off the hook and admit
my responsibility for my feelings
and my actions.

495

You will just naturally be an obsessive maniac if you are not working with God every second of every day.

496

For the person I am, with all of my failings, God has been unbelievably, incredibly kind to me.

497

When God talks, He talks through people who have been through the same problems we have been through. It is worth listening.

498

There is no such thing
as a life without problems.
The only variable is our serenity.

499

Laughter is sacrosanct.
Laughter is sacred and lifesaving,
especially laughter at ourselves.

500

If my day is not going right,
it's not worth worrying about a lot.
It's definitely going God's way.

501

Here is a test of the basics of life:
What I want is my will. What happens
is God's will. It is smart to accept this,
and more than smart . . . it is vital.

502

The great secret is that everything
is going to turn out all right.
Now you know it.

503

I don't have to be a genius. I don't
have to be Einstein. I just have
to go through my day.

504

Whether or not you "count"
depends on who does the counting.
To God you count just as much as
anyone else. No more and no less.

505

You throw yourself out there
and see what happens.

506

Any small problem can become
a big problem if we just dwell on it.

507

There is no excuse
not to forgive.

508

Whatever is going to happen
will happen in God's time, and it is
not at all clear that God works on
the same timetable we work on.

509

Do not look for the
payoff in "doing."
The payoff is in "being."

510

Worrying about how
others feel about me is not a good
or useful employment of my time.

511

The journey is now. Every stop
on the journey is surrender if you
play your cards right.

512

There is only one Superhero.

513

A serene heart
is a first-class ticket
through my day.

514

Life is like a rough diamond:
Polish it with faith.

515

Peace of mind is the
only true wealth. It is worth
hearing over and over again.

516

If we can triumph over fear,
we can triumph over anything.
This must be our quest.

517

There is no such thing
as defeat when we are not
fighting God's will.

518

Courage is walking with
God even when you are afraid.

519

Just resting and staying calm
will solve most of my problems.

520

Prayer is my drug of choice.
Forgiveness is my drug of choice.
Surrender is my drug of choice.

521

Fear is the
most paralytic
disease.

522

Faith is the
miracle antidote to fear.

523

It's always going
to be one darned thing or another.

524

I don't want a ticket to
"Tomorrowland." I am happy
with a ticket to Todayland.

525

Thank you, God, for reminding
me that I don't have to listen
to my head all day long.

526

Today I have
an incredible gift:
I have today.

527

Thank you, God, for helping
me learn that I will always
have unresolved
problems.

528

Don't believe everything
the special prosecutor inside
your head tells you.

529

You do not have
to hurt yourself even
if you want to.

530

Behold the sheer unimaginable
gift of being alive right in
the here-and-now.

About the Author

Ben Stein is a lawyer, economist, writer, actor, teacher, and former game-show host (his show *Win Ben Stein's Money* won seven Emmys). He lives in Southern California with his wife, Alexandra; his son, Thomas; and many dogs and cats. He is very active in fund-raising for animal-rights and children's-rights charities in Los Angeles and throughout the country.

Website: **www.benstein.com**

Hay House Titles
of Related Interest

BOOKS

Eliminating Stress, Finding Inner Peace
(book-with-CD), by Brian L. Weiss, M.D.

Everyday Wisdom, by Dr. Wayne W. Dyer

Five Steps for Overcoming Fear and Self-Doubt,
by Wyatt Webb

Heart Thoughts, by Louise L. Hay

Wisdom of the Heart, by Alan Cohen

CARD DECKS

Attitude Is Everything™ *Cards,* by Keith Harrell

Empowerment Cards, by Tavis Smiley

Heart and Soul, by Sylvia Browne

Inner Peace Cards, by Dr. Wayne W. Dyer

The Teachings of Abraham Well-Being Cards,
by Esther and Jerry Hicks

PERPETUAL FLIP CALENDARS

Everyday Wisdom, by Dr. Wayne W. Dyer

The Power of Intention, by Dr. Wayne W. Dyer

Wise Words—compiled from New Dimensions® radio
interviews by Michael Toms

A Year of Daily Wisdom, by Marianne Williamson

All of the above are available at your local
bookstore, or may be ordered by visiting:
Hay House USA: **www.hayhouse.com**
Hay House Australia: **www.hayhouse.com.au**
Hay House UK: **www.hayhouse.co.uk**
Hay House South Africa: **orders@psdprom.co.za**

We hope you enjoyed this Hay House book.
If you'd like to receive a free catalog featuring additional
Hay House books and products, or if you'd like information
about the Hay Foundation, please contact:

Hay House, Inc., P.O. Box 5100, Carlsbad, CA 92018-5100

(760) 431-7695 or **(800) 654-5126**
(760) 431-6948 (fax) or **(800) 650-5115 (fax)**
www.hayhouse.com

Published and distributed in Australia by:
Hay House Australia Pty. Ltd. • 18/36 Ralph St. • Alexandria
NSW 2015 • *Phone:* 612-9669-4299 • *Fax:* 612-9669-4144
www.hayhouse.com.au

Published and distributed in the United Kingdom by:
Hay House UK, Ltd. • Unit 62, Canalot Studios • 222 Kensal Rd.,
London W10 5BN • *Phone:* 44-20-8962-1230
Fax: 44-20-8962-1239 • www.hayhouse.co.uk

Published and distributed in the Republic of South Africa by:
Hay House SA (Pty), Ltd., P.O. Box 990, Witkoppen 2068
Phone/Fax: 2711-7012233 • orders@psdprom.co.za

Distributed in Canada by:
Raincoast • 9050 Shaughnessy St., Vancouver, B.C. V6P 6E5
Phone: (604) 323-7100 • *Fax:* (604) 323-2600

Sign up via the Hay House USA Website to receive the Hay House
online newsletter and stay informed about what's going on with your
favorite authors. You'll receive bimonthly announcements about:
Discounts and Offers, Special Events, Product Highlights,
Free Excerpts, Giveaways, and more!
www.hayhouse.com